Summary of

Smarter Faster Better

by Charles Duhigg

Instaread

Instaread on Smarter Faster Better by Charles Duhigg

Please Note

This is a summary with analysis.

Copyright © 2016 by Instaread. All rights reserved worldwide. No part of this publication may be reproduced or transmitted in any form without the prior written consent of the publisher.

Limit of Liability/Disclaimer of Warranty: The publisher and author make no representations or warranties with respect to the accuracy or completeness of these contents and disclaim all warranties such as warranties of fitness for a particular purpose. The author or publisher is not liable for any damages whatsoever. The fact that an individual or organization is referred to in this document as a citation or source of information does not imply that the author or publisher endorses the information that the individual or organization provided. This concise summary is unofficial and is not authorized, approved, licensed, or endorsed by the original book's author or publisher.

Table of Contents

Overview 4

Important People 6

Key Takeaways 8

Analysis 11

Key Takeaway 1 11

Key Takeaway 2 13

Key Takeaway 3 15

Key Takeaway 4 17

Key Takeaway 5 19

Key Takeaway 6 21

Key Takeaway 7 23

Key Takeaway 8 24

Key Takeaway 9 26

Author's Style 28

Author's Perspective 30

References 32

Overview

Smarter Faster Better by Charles Duhigg is a scientifically grounded self-help book that describes ways to increase productivity. Duhigg relates stories about ways to encourage individuals to make decisions and assign their own significant meanings to them, demonstrating that making choices and knowing the meaning of those choices stimulates further action and motivation. Analyses of team productivity programs and the functioning of effective teams show that productive teams should be diverse, call on every team member to participate, and create a safe environment for team members.

The best way for teams to set goals is to work toward a stretch goal that also meets the five SMART criteria: the stretch goal should be specific, measurable, achievable, realistic, and based on a set timeline. A set of stretch goals can be achieved with total effort. Those goals should be meaningful and should not distract from the need for new goals when circumstances change, as in a crisis. The brain will try to focus only on one thing in a crisis, a phenomenon called psychological tunneling, which has caused plane crashes. Reversing this trend requires visualizing worst-case scenarios to prepare for their possible emergence.

Manufacturing and development methods such as both Lean and Agile move decision-making powers to the people closest to the problem, preventing resources from being tied up in bureaucracy. The development of the Federal Bureau of Investigation's Sentinel program and a case study about an automotive factory that returned power to the workers, resulting in productivity gains, demonstrate that these methods can apply to a variety of circumstances.

Decision-making based on predictions should use models that incorporate multiple probabilities, consider the potential profit or loss of the decisions, and embrace the unknown. Sometimes the best way to drive data understanding is to make the data harder to understand at first. This strategy, called data disfluency, requires people to handle data in an inefficient way. Some of the most creative modern minds are actually brokers who combine two previously established ideas in creative ways. Creativity also thrives under tension, such as a deadline or a sudden change in environment.

Instaread on Smarter Faster Better by Charles Duhigg

Important People

Charles Duhigg is a *New York Times* reporter who won a Pulitzer Prize for explanatory journalism for a series on Apple. He has written two self-help books, *The Power of Habit* (2012) and *Smarter Better Faster* (2016).

Annie Duke is a professional poker player and a previous leader in total winnings among women in the World Series of Poker.

Lorne Michaels is the creator and producer of *Saturday Night Live*, producer of *Late Night*, executive producer of *30 Rock*, and executive producer of *The Tonight Show*.

Eli Zeira was the major general of the Israel Defense Forces and the director of Israeli military intelligence until he was found negligent of his duty for failure to respond to troop movements prior to the Yom Kippur War.

Pierre-Cedric Bonin was the pilot of Air France Flight 447, which crashed into the Atlantic Ocean in June 2009 as a result of apparent pilot error.

Julia Rozovsky is a people analytics manager at Google.

Chad Fulgham is a cyber security expert who was the chief information officer at the FBI until 2012. He is the co-founder and chairman of consulting firm PerCredo LLC.

Chris Buck directed the animated films *Tarzan* and *Frozen* at Disney, and *Surf's Up* at Sony Pictures.

Jennifer Lee co-wrote the Disney film *Wreck-It Ralph* and co-directed *Frozen*.

Key Takeaways

1. Motivation results from the individual's belief in the power to make choices and control outcomes. The motivation to accomplish difficult things comes from the meaning behind those choices.

2. The most productive teams actively seek each member's input, have defined rules and goals, trust one another, and feel safe in proposing ideas to each other.

3. Cognitive tunneling is the misdirection of focus during a crisis. A mental model of what to do in a crisis and visualization of the problem can prevent tunneling on the wrong things.

4. Set goals that include hard to accomplish "stretch" goals, and make certain that they are specific, measurable, achievable, realistic, and based on a set timeline.

5. Decision-making power is best given to the people closest to the problem. When they are entrusted with power, their commitment to the team increases, making the whole operation more successful.

6. Models to predict the future should be constructed through a combination of probabilities relevant to the situation, avoid the bias of

focusing on successes, factor in the potential earnings and losses in the probabilities, and incorporate the unknown.

7. Creative brokers create new things by combining established ideas in unconventional ways.

8. Creativity can be motivated by tension and change, either through the creative desperation resulting from a deadline, or an intermediate disturbance in the status quo.

9. Forcing inefficient interactions with data can increase comprehension of it through disfluency, as does encouraging interaction through testing hypotheses.

Thank you for purchasing this Instaread book

Download the Instaread mobile app to get unlimited text & audio summaries of bestselling books.

Visit Instaread.co to learn more.

Analysis

Key Takeaway 1

Motivation results from the individual's belief in the power to make choices and control outcomes. The motivation to accomplish difficult things comes from the meaning behind those choices.

Analysis

Making decisions is one way to improve the motivation to accomplish challenging tasks. When Marines train to push their bodies to their limits, they are encouraged to set their own agendas and ask each other why they want to do such difficult things, which helps create a deeper meaning for their tasks. In preliminary findings, forced decision-making also hastened recovery for individuals suffering from a type of brain damage that destroys internal motivation.

Applying the concept of motivation driven by decision-making to a life goal, such as embarking on a globe-crossing adventure, involves first making a single decision about the adventure, a decision intended to kick-start more decisions and more progress. Before Roz Savage began setting records as the first woman to make Atlantic, Pacific, and Indian Ocean crossings by canoe, she worked for a management consultancy. Her adventure began with an exercise to determine what she would need to do to live the life she wanted. Savage then decided to put rowing across the Atlantic Ocean at the top of her priority list and started planning her trip as a hypothetical exercise. These initial decisions made it easier to accomplish her goals. It took just 14 months between her first decision and her first ocean crossing. [1]

Key Takeaway 2

The most productive teams actively seek each member's input, have defined rules and goals, trust one another, and feel safe in proposing ideas to each other.

Analysis

Two teams demonstrate the shape of successful teams in business. The first is Google's employees, which the company learned are best served in diverse groups that are not competing internally and instead trust each other. The second team is the original cast and writers for *Saturday Night Live*. Although the *SNL* team was not without drama, they encouraged each other to follow through with ideas and avoided shooting each other down.

Different individuals might join the board of a charter school with different ideas about how the school should be run. Those conflicting ideas can prevent the board from attaining trust and psychological safety by maintaining a critical environment in which few people make suggestions. For example, if the board began with a core group that trusted each other, and then added outsiders who are unfamiliar and have not yet earned the group's trust, the original members might exclude the new members from informal, but important brainstorming sessions out of fear that the newcomers might criticize their ideas. As a result, the new members would fail to learn how to trust the original members, and a rift would develop that would decrease the whole board's sense of unity and sabotage their productivity by causing members to withhold valid ideas. In another scenario, if the board is composed of some members who want to trust each other and one person who is more interested in personal advancement than in a successful school, the self-interested person could be enough of a toxic influence to prevent everyone else from developing trust for the group.

Key Takeaway 3

Cognitive tunneling is the misdirection of focus during a crisis. A mental model of what to do in a crisis and visualization of the problem can prevent tunneling on the wrong things.

Analysis

In the course of everyday life, the mind's focus is spread broadly, but during a crisis that focus is narrowly directed, sometimes on things that are not directly connected to the crisis. For airplane pilots, the cognitive tunneling that occurs during a crisis can lead to focusing on the wrong solution, resulting in a crash. They can avoid such tunneling by training themselves to look in the right place for a solution and visualizing their situation along the way.

Cognitive tunneling may have its origins in evolutionary advances in the ancient human brain. For example, early humans had to react quickly if they encountered a predator when foraging for food, triggering a response known as fight-or-flight. During this response, the body releases adrenaline into the bloodstream, increases blood pressure and heart rate, and redirects blood flow away from areas such as the skin and digestive tract toward the muscles needed to escape from danger. The feeling of panic that these involuntary physiological responses create may be responsible, to some degree, for cognitive tunneling. It makes sense that while the body is narrowing the focus of its resources to only the most necessary functions, it is also changing the use of resources in the brain to narrow focus on the threat and ignore everything else, such as a minor ache or hunger. [2] In the modern world, that narrow focus can cut out things that would normally be helpful in a crisis, like the instrument panels in the plane, unless the individual has already developed the habit to focus on the instrument panels while the acute stress response is occurring.

Key Takeaway 4

Set goals that include hard to accomplish "stretch" goals, and make certain that they are specific, measurable, achievable, realistic, and based on a set timeline.

Analysis

Goals that are too difficult to be possible or too ordinary to be meaningful do not increase productivity. Instead, goals should be challenging and should have a deeper meaning than everything else on the to-do list. Those goals should also follow the guidelines represented by the acronym SMART: They should be specific, measurable, achievable, realistic, and follow a timeline.

In personal life, a man's SMART goal might be losing 30 pounds of body weight before his wedding. That goal is only realistic if it allows the man to lose the weight at a safe rate, which experts usually state is one to two pounds per week. That sets the realistic timeline for losing 30 pounds, requiring 15 to 30 weeks with a measurable goal of one to two pounds per week. Achieving that goal requires cutting 500 to 1,000 daily calories. This can be achieved by giving up soft drinks and sugar-loaded coffee drinks, eating a small serving of fruit rather than a dessert, cutting portions at restaurants in half, and reversing a mindless snacking habit. Exercise can also contribute to that calorie-cutting goal by burning calories. [3] So the complete SMART goal would be to lose 30 pounds in 15 weeks by cutting 500 calories from food and burning 500 calories in exercise every day, thereby achieving a loss of two pounds per week in order to fit into an ideal wedding outfit.

Key Takeaway 5

Decision-making power is best given to the people closest to the problem. When they are entrusted with power, their commitment to the team increases, making the whole operation more successful.

Analysis

The FBI learned to adopt an Agile or Lean production method from a consultant who applied the method to the FBI's Sentinel project. The development team that was given control of the project completed it in two years and used a fraction of its budget. A joint venture between automakers General Motors and Toyota similarly revealed that giving workers control of the assembly line, stopping it when necessary, resulted in a better product and more commitment from the workers.

These methods are becoming popular in manufacturing and technology, but they can be applied to any industry where workers are closer to delay-causing problems than supervisors are. For example, if a woman running a restaurant wanted to improve the presentation of food and was concerned that the waitstaff and cooks were not committed to the company, she might give them the power to decide when a dish looks nice enough to serve. A waiter might not take a dish to a customer if it looks messy, and a chef might use the newly bestowed power over presentation to suggest new methods of keeping plates clean and placing sauces on the plates. If the kitchen staff members all learn to enjoy sending beautiful dishes to customers, their pride in their work prevents others at the restaurant from not taking their commitments seriously.

Key Takeaway 6

Models to predict the future should be constructed through a combination of probabilities relevant to the situation, avoid the bias of focusing on successes, factor in the potential earnings and losses in the probabilities, and incorporate the unknown.

Analysis

Building predictive models of the future is more complicated than finding the probability of a single event. The circumstances and environment of the event, the potential loss or gain from making a prediction, and unbiased examples are all necessary to build an accurate model.

As is necessary in team productivity, motivation, and goal-setting, commitment is also useful in creating more accurate predictions. The Good Judgment Project run by the Intelligence Advanced Research Projects Activity determined that accurate forecasters tend not to believe in fate or destiny, reject dogmatic thinking, are willing to test their hypotheses, and might change their views if they are wrong.

While all the math that goes into probability calculations may be intimidating, the Good Judgment Project's most accurate forecasters, called superforecasters, were seldom mathematicians or statisticians already, though they had an understanding of the significance of a change in a few percentage points. According to poker player and risk analyst Aaron Brown, appreciating the difference between a 55/45 proposition and a 45/55 proposition is what makes a great poker player. [4] With better predictions, an individual can develop better road maps for future projects and anticipate obstacles that could hinder success and productivity.

Key Takeaway 7

Creative brokers create new things by combining established ideas in unconventional ways.

Analysis

Some of the most creative ideas are not entirely original, but come from the combination of two or more established ideas that had not been combined before. For the writers of *West Side Story*, that combination was about gang violence, the William Shakespeare play *Romeo and Juliet*, and choreographed dance.

In the food industry, interesting fusions of existing cuisines are popular because they combine common threads between different types of cooking with unusual combinations that would not result from a single national cuisine. For example, Korean taco trucks combine two cuisines with some common elements, such as spicy sauces, cilantro, and grilled meats like pork and chicken. [5]

Key Takeaway 8

Creativity can be motivated by tension and change, either through the creative desperation resulting from a deadline, or an intermediate disturbance in the status quo.

Analysis

During the writing process for *Frozen*, writers came across their best ideas when their original ideas were already considered and turned down. They had limited time left to finish their project, and that tension resulted in the most productive brainstorming sessions. They also came across their best ideas after one of the writers was promoted to be a director, giving her a different perspective on the project and changing the other writers' relationships with her and the other director.

For an individual doing something less dependent on artistic creativity than developing a movie, such as finding a solution to a marketing dilemma, similar strategies that create tension or change the environment can still be useful. For example, brainstorming sessions can require five ideas from each team member within five minutes. A marketing director can give the team an artificially short deadline for a project, knowing that the deadline can be extended once they come across a good plan, or the same director might withhold a particular resource from the team until they come up with a plan for how to use it efficiently. Promoting an employee or shuffling the power hierarchy can cause intermediate disturbances for a team. For an individual, making a similar disturbance could involve finding a new place to work for a day, changing the music that plays in the office, or going out to have a new experience on the weekend before returning to work with refreshed concepts from which to draw.

Key Takeaway 9

Forcing inefficient interactions with data can increase comprehension of it through disfluency, as does encouraging interaction through testing hypotheses.

Analysis

Making data easy to absorb can actually make people less likely to spend the necessary time studying it and interacting with it. A better strategy is to make the data complicated or have the team members make the data set themselves, so that they learn more about its structure and possibilities.

One way to implement this concept in the business world would be to write fewer short memos and emails. If the information that workers need is located within a much longer report or multi-page communications, they have no choice but to carefully read more of the document in order to find the details they need. Forcing employees to confront less precise communications also means they must devote focused attention to the document, which will prevent distracted replies and encourage less hurried and more thoughtful responses.

In personal life, improving comprehension of a book might involve reading it in paper format and forcing oneself to interact with the book by highlighting important passages, folding pages with interesting quotes, or writing those quotes into a notebook. Since interactivity can also result in greater comprehension, a reader might decide to read for the purpose of testing an idea, such as whether men or women have more spoken lines in the book. That task would require extra work in the form of recording the locations of lines, marking who said them, and tallying them up at the end of the book.

Author's Style

Charles Duhigg writes in an authoritative style and often refers to scientific studies, offers anecdotes from the business and government sectors, and provides advice for the reader. Most chapters begin with an anecdote, told as a story in chronological order without any insight into the eventual lesson to learn from it. Before finishing the anecdote, and usually at a crucial decision point, Duhigg jumps into another anecdote from a different time or place, again told chronologically with no insight into the connection between the two or the purpose of introducing the second anecdote. The anecdotes are resolved at the end of the chapter and tied together by common themes or findings. Along the way, Duhigg introduces more scientific studies, historical examples, and character descriptions.

The lessons delivered in anecdotes are usually supported by scientific studies and sometimes conclude with an explicitly stated piece of advice for the reader to apply those findings to become more productive. The anecdotes and studies are generally from recent history, and they do not involve Duhigg personally except for the appendix, which outlines the ways Duhigg used the lessons he wrote about in the process of writing the book.

On occasion, Duhigg describes with certainty events which he admits in the anecdote or in the endnotes he could not know for sure. For example, he describes in vivid detail the events surrounding a kidnapping but writes in the endnote that no one involved in the crime or the investigation would reply to his queries. He also writes with certainty about the reasons that an Air France pilot caused his plane to stall and crash into the ocean, although the causes he describes cannot be known for certain.

Most scientific terms and technical language are defined for the reader and the language is generally not very complicated. For example, Duhigg thoroughly explains the impact of damage to the brain's striatum and the mechanical systems within airplanes. However, he does not explain concepts such as the full extent of profit and loss probabilities in poker or what an Erlang distribution is.

Author's Perspective

Charles Duhigg is a reporter known for his ability to explain complicated topics to the audience, as evidenced by the Pulitzer Prize he won with the staff of the *New York Times* for explanatory journalism on the widespread influence of Apple and its devices. His first book, *The Power of Habit* (2012), was a similarly structured examination of the formation, uses, and manipulation of habits, including scientific studies, anecdotes, and some personal experiences alongside explicit advice for the reader. As a *New York Times* reporter, Duhigg has written about the 2008 financial crisis, water quality, and investors who take advantage of seniors to make a profit.

~~~~ **END OF INSTAREAD** ~~~~

Thank you for purchasing this Instaread book

Download the Instaread mobile app to get unlimited text & audio summaries of bestselling books.

Visit Instaread.co to learn more.

References

1. Savage, Roz. "Why Row Across The Oceans?" *TED Radio Hour*. Episode: "To The Edge." July 26, 2013. Accessed April 7, 2016. http://www.npr.org/2013/07/11/201092483/to-the-edge

2. Schocker, Laura. "This Is Your Body On Stress." *Huffpost Healthy Living*. April 5, 2013. Accessed March 23, 2016. http://www.huffingtonpost.com/2013/03/19/body-stress-response_n_2902073.html

3. Centers for Disease Control and Prevention. "What is healthy weight loss?" Division of Nutrition, Physical Activity, and Obesity. Accessed March 23, 2016. http://www.cdc.gov/healthyweight/losing_weight/index.html

4. Dubner, Stephen. "How to Be Less Terrible at Predicting the Future." *Freakonomics Radio*. January 14, 2016. Accessed March 23, 2016. http://freakonomics.com/podcast/how-to-be-less-terrible-at-predicting-the-future-a-new-freakonomics-radio-podcast/

5. Edge, John. "The Tortilla Takes a Road Trip to Korea." *The New York Times*. July 27, 2010. Accessed March 23, 2016. http://www.nytimes.com/2010/07/28/dining/28united.html?pagewanted=all&_r=1

CPSIA information can be obtained
at www.ICGtesting.com
Printed in the USA
LVOW01s2201220616
493679LV00036B/633/P